Mingling Voices

SERIES EDITOR: MANIJEH MANNANI

Give us wholeness, for we are broken
But who are we asking, and why do we ask?
  Phyllis Webb

National in scope, Mingling Voices draws on the work of both new and established novelists, short story tellers, and poets. The series especially, but not exclusively, aims to promote authors who challenge traditions and cultural stereotypes. It is designed to reach a wide variety of readers, both generalists and specialists. Mingling Voices is also open to literary works that delineate the immigrant experience in Canada.

Series Titles

Poems for a Small Park
by E.D. Blodgett

Dreamwork
by Jonathan Locke Hart

Windfall Apples: Tanka and Kyoka
by Richard Stevenson

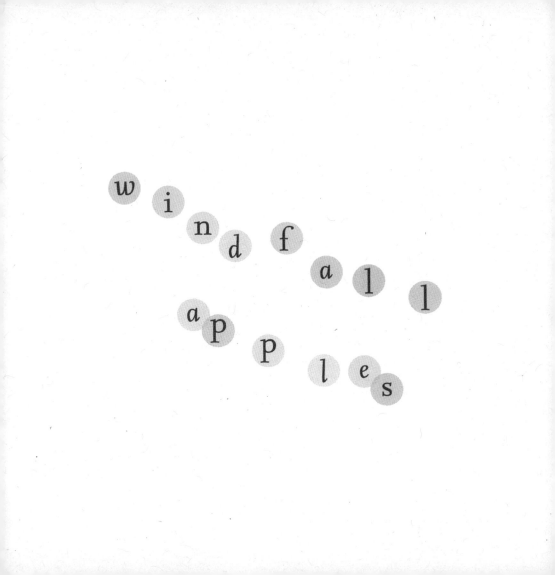

windfall apples

Windfall Apples

TANKA AND KYOKA

by Richard Stevenson

AU PRESS
Athabasca University

(C) 2010 Richard Stevenson

Library and Archives Canada Cataloguing in Publication

Stevenson, Richard, 1952–

Windfall apples : tanka and kyoka / Richard Stevenson.

(Mingling voices, ISSN 1917-9405)
Also available in electronic format (978-1-897425-89-3).
ISBN 978-1-897425-88-6

1. Waka, Canadian (English). I. Title. II. Series: Mingling voices

PS8587.T479W61 2010   C811'.54   C2010-900901-0

Published by AU Press,
Athabasca University
1200, 10011 – 109 Street
Edmonton, AB T5J 3S8

Cover and book design
by Natalie Olsen,
www.kisscutdesign.com

Printed and bound in Canada
by Marquis Book Printing.

A volume in the
Mingling Voices series:
ISSN 1917-9405 (Print)
ISSN 1917-9413 (Online)

Acknowledgements

Poems in this collection have previously appeared in or been accepted for the following e-zines, journals, and small press publications:

American Tanka, Ascent Aspirations, Ash Moon Anthology: Poems on Aging in Modern English Tanka (Modern English Tanka Press, 2008), Atlas Poetica, Baby Clam, Bottle Rockets, Germination (mytown.ca), Gusts, Haiku Presence, Hutt, Kaleidowhirl Literary Journal, Lynx, Nisqually Delta Review, Rags, Regina Weese, Ribbons (American Tanka Society), Simply Haiku, Snow Monkey, Streetlights: Poetry of Urban Life in Modern English Tanka (Modern English Tanka Press, 2009), Take Five: Best Contemporary Tanka (Modern English Tanka Press, 2008), Twaddle Magazine, World Haiku Review, and Writing the Land: Alberta Through Its Poets (House of Blue Skies, 2007).

"Riding the Dragon" also appeared in my earlier collection of haiku, senryu, and tanka, *A Charm of Finches* (Ekstasis Editions, 2004).

Thanks to the editors, many who have published me issue after issue, for their continued support. Thanks to my family too for putting up with my haikoodling.

For my new nuclear unit, Gepke, Marika, Adrian, Kelly, and Kyle — the perfect passel of brats; our growing clowder of cats — Max, Smokey, Sushi, and Earle (a.k.a. Leddy Headbutter); and our wonderful wacky duo, Oscar, miniature action dachshund, and Cosmo, cyborg golden retriever and most excellent mellow yellow fellow. May we continue to rock in the free world.

Thanks too to "the Nelson Family" and my good friends in Lethbridge and on the Web: you all make my creative life possible. Paddles up!

Introduction

Tradition, innovation and playfulness are an important part of poetry. Poems express a range of feelings in multifold forms that might try to overturn time or misfortune, or chase away tedium and make the spirit more nimble. Richard Stevenson combines tradition, innovation and playfulness, and reaches back through the centuries and brings the Japanese poetic forms of *tanka* and *kyoka* to life in twenty-first century North America. He translates these poetic forms through time and space and gives them a contemporary feel.

As Richard Stevenson is using Japanese forms in his poems in English, it is important to say a few things about the established and later forms of Japanese poetry. Tradition is a key to established forms. The *waka* flourished in the Heian period, when the aristocracy ruled and were composing *waka* with enthusiasm, about the time the *Tale of Genji* was produced, and before the samurai came to power. This *waka* is the thirty-one-syllable form now referred to as *tanka*, which is arranged in five lines of 5-7-5-7-7.[1] Poems in Japanese came to be written by the samurai and many others as in time more people could read and write and produce literature.

This continuity and change in Japanese poetics is something that Stevenson draws on. In Japanese poetry, new poetic genres came into being during the Edo period (1600–1868). These forms were popular linked verse (*haikai renga*, which included the *hokku*, later renamed *haiku*), *kyoka* (wild Japanese poetry), *kyoshi* (wild Chinese poetry) and *senryu* (satiric or humorous seventeen-syllable poetry).[2] *Kyoka* were Japanese poems that did not conform to the prescribed norms of *waka* imagery and diction. *Kyoka* had existed since the eighth century, but *waka* purists often turned up their noses at them. Still, *kyoka* were increasingly popular in the late medieval period (sixteenth century).[3] This trend continued into the Edo period, which involved a keen interest in *kyoka* during the late eighteenth century and the publication of many *kyoka* collections. The *kyoka* of the Edo period may be viewed as the unorthodox and unconventional counterparts to *waka*, and a similar relation existed between *kyoshi* and *kanshi* (Chinese poetry) and between *senryu* and *haikai* (haiku).[4] *Kyoka* poets of the Edo period came from a wide range of social backgrounds, including aristocrats, samurai and urban commoners.[5] According to Haruo Shirane, "[t]he humour of *kyoka* derives from placing something vulgar, low, or mundane in an elegant Japanese form or context."[6] In this sense, *kyoka* exemplify the tendency in the Edo period towards the juxtaposition of high and low culture. This technique often veered into parody. As Shirane says, "[i]n contrast to *senryu*, which flourished at the same time as *kyoka* and remains popular today, *kyoka* as a genre did not last into the modern period. Although in the late eighteenth century it eventually spread beyond the sphere of educated samurai and aristocrats to commoners, it still required a knowledge of the classical poetic tradition, which made it difficult for commoner audiences to appreciate."[7] When Japanese poetic forms become the inspiration of English poetry, then translation, adaptation and differences in time and place come into play. This brief background of Japanese poetry highlights the tradition Stevenson has gone to and how he has followed and departed from it. He has blended tradition, renewal and innovation in suggestive ways. Stevenson makes use of the serious and humorous, and translates these forms into English and into a new time and context.

Windfall Apples is a full-length collection of tanka and kyoka. The tanka is a serious and mannered poem of feeling and suggestiveness, often about nature, and composed within the confines of a brief and demanding form. Stevenson uses the form of the Japanese-language tanka, but plays with its form. He treats the tanka as an experiment in images and imagistic poetry and expresses a wide array of subjects, including his life in western Canada. Kyoka, poems in the tanka form of five lines, might be called anti-*tanka* poems because they appear to be less serious, more humorous.[8] With its often political and social content, the *kyoka* tends to be sardonic and ironic. It can parody the *waka* and use slang. The *kyoka* also echoes *senryu* in its thematic preoccupation with human nature. Stevenson goes to the traditions of *tanka* and *kyoka* to create his book, but the boundary between them changes as they are rendered into English.

Following the conventions of *tanka* and *kyoka* in Japanese poetry, Stevenson uses powerful images in his poems and evokes a range of feelings in *Windfall Apples*. The forms he chooses are compact and require grace and the appearance of effortlessness. He creates a world of the domestic and everyday:

> magpie and grackle —
> who's the sauciest?
> cats with piqued ears
> and quivering noses
> want to know

There is a noise in these lines, a quiet listening in anticipation, and a kind of potential action on the brink of realization. Another scene shows the relation between the human and natural worlds. It leaves suspended the tension between them:

> febrile web —
> my wife's angry talk
> with my daughter
> shakes the raindrops
> off a branch

The readers follow the fever of the connection and wonder whether the talk could shake the branch; in a sense, they are led to accept the compact supposition of this small fictional world.

Nature is, of course, a key to the imagery in many of the most beautiful poems in this collection. There is a lightness of touch and a power of observation that lead the readers through the light, the shadow and the feel of the natural realm:

> the emerald hour —
> that time when the grass
> is its deepest green,
> cottonwoods whisper
> what the wind knows

Another poem reaches beyond the bounds of the poem itself:

> at the farthest reach
> of my watering
> hose stream
> a cabbage white
> flutters a while

From the "while" to the "white," the stream flutters into space. There are a number of other instances, but I do not wish to give too much away, as part of what these short poems do is compress and surprise.

Stevenson is able to blend these moments with the frictions and potential violence, the frustrations and fascinations of the everyday. This is a poetic world of tension between the ordinary and extraordinary, the rough and delicate. This disjunction involves the reader and gives the collection part of its drama. Here, between word and action, the poetry unfolds. Taking ancient forms of Japanese literature of a time far from the democratic and popular world of the prairie and other land-scapes, Stevenson gives them his own vernacular, that of the place he dwells in, the places he visits and knows. He observes and translates the daily turns of a life now into an art that connects the readers with this and other worlds.

Windfall Apples makes an important technical contribution to English-language poetry written in the Japanese style in Canada. It is versatile and the author knows what he wants to do. These poems combine a fluidity of expression with an accessible world for the contemporary reader. Richard Stevenson combines East and West in a suggestive typology. English has long been a dance of many times and places, and is becoming more so all the time. Poems in English, especially those that draw on other languages, forms and literatures, are sites of innovation and interest. Stevenson's *tanka* and *kyoka* make a contribution to that way forward: they look elsewhere and back, to make the here and now something new and remarkable, something to look forward to.

Jonathan Hart
January 2010

ACKNOWLEDGEMENTS

I would like to thank Dr. Anne Commons and Shelina Brown for their advice and comments on Japanese poetry and culture, and from saving me from some embarrassing generalizations and other slips. Their wisdom is reflected in the main text and the notes, particularly Anne Commons in most notes, and Shelina Brown in notes 2 and 8. Anne Commons also clarified for me the relation between *waka* and the later forms, and called my attention to these matters in Shirane, as reflected in the main text.

1 The most admired classical *waka*, in the thirty-one-syllable form, date mainly from the period of 905–1205 A.D. (Anne Commons, personal communication).

2 In Japanese, a *hokku* or *haiku* always has to feature a seasonal reference: it is one of the conventions of the form (Anne Commons, personal communication). A seventeen-syllable Japanese poem without a season word is a *senryu*, not a *haiku*, regardless of its content. This seasonal requirement does not always seem to apply to *haiku* written in English. Thus, many English "*haiku*" would be considered *senryu* in Japanese. The term *haiku* was coined in the nineteenth century. Haiku, a more popular form in English — as a translation or carrying across into English — is also a word invented to renew hokku (Shelina Brown, personal communication), which was originally the opening stanza of a *renga* (linked poem) but came to be a poem that stood on its own. The *haiku* does not rhyme. It contains an image or feeling in two parts over three lines. There are 5 syllables in the first verse line, 7 in the second, and 5 in the last.

3 Inukai Kiyoshi et al., ed., *Waka Daijiten* [Large Dictionary of Waka] (Tokyo: Meiji shoin, 1986), p.226.

4 Haruo Shirane, *Early Modern Japanese Literature: An Anthology, 1600–1900* (New York: Columbia University Press, 2002), p.528.

5 Ibid.

6 Ibid.

7 Ibid.

8 Kyu suggests a lewd, crazy, lascivious, humorous poem (Shelina Brown, personal communication).

lawn so green
it looks like the tree
is drinking it
through a straw —
teenagers attached

magpie and grackle —
who's the sauciest?
cats with piqued ears
and quivering noses
want to know

yellow-mantled,
a friend informs us —
marmot of the plains.
three floors up, appendix gone,
your incision's stapled grin.

hum babe! hum babe!
the gimped pigeon's swollen foot
a punched baseball glove:
you want to toss a ball
when its foot falls off

church rally —
boy finds his dental plate
under the bleachers,
gives me
a big window grin

Victoria —
a mallard coasting
in for a landing
hits black ice,
skitters down the pond

it's a tree, isn't it?
decorated maybe, but
where else would I piss?
dog's soft brown eyes and arched brow
offer both of us relief

febrile web —
my wife's angry talk
with my daughter
shakes the raindrops
off a branch

a roller coaster —
or so it seems, the way
these kids' eyes
hold the curves of the
new computer game

Kimberly T-shirt:
silhouette cartoon couple
in the cross hairs.
If it's tourist season,
how come we can't shoot a few?

blonde on blonde —
not Dylan's masterpiece
but a retriever
on grass I refuse
to water any more

she's not in the mood —
though the day lilies'
orange megaphones
announce their readiness
to anything with six legs

Issa schmissa —
how many bytes of data
did you take away
from my computer
today, friend ant?

Backyard Jazz:
A Tanka Suite

retriever pants —
pitter patter sprinkler splash —
so gone a day
he's blonde on blonde, baby,
hunkers his honey ass down!

    *

cabbage white's
got a hip hop beat,
sizzles wing and stick
on the cymbal of each
sprinkled leaf

    *

dachshund's so down
on the store-bought bone
he's prone too, you bet.
the deep green glove of the day
ready for the sun to drop in....

*

meow, baby!
cat's on the table
and he don't need Mabel —
bites my knuckle
away from my beer

*

old ginger —
your own jar of
unopened marmalade.
what's under those lids
on such a hot day?

ash in the pipe —
grass a deeper green
in the shade,
the retriever appraises me
with his one good eye

twenty O mouths,
heads like eggs
in a carton:
Guns and Hoses capsize
turning into their own wake

(Lethbridge Rotary Dragonboat Festival)

newly varnished,
the old wicker headboard
now a trellis
for a Merlot vine,
rosary of water beads

Canada Day —
fireworks cancelled on account
of storm conditions,
but what a fireworks display
the spirea blooms make!

the emerald hour —
that time when the grass
is its deepest green,
cottonwoods whisper
what the wind knows

as if to say
my turf, my nest,
hawk's insistent cry
reeled off at each
and every tree

Kibbles and Bits
flushed out of the car
hood and air ducts?
ah, dead mouse smell
from the air conditioner

our dachshund won't eat.
sixteen hundred clams later,
the vet presents
a shoelace, bits of plastic,
a swatch of towel

sorry, hummingbird
for the loud colours
of my Hawaiian shirt,
the thrum of your tiny wings
so soft I might have missed you

finally some sun —
I don't know what's worse:
the sound of the lawn mowers
or this damn mosquito
fueling up before take-off

nothing erratic
about the placement
of this boulder —
not after two cars
through the fence

(for Brian Bartlett)

dachshund's frantic:
the new kitten has vanished.
toenails telegraph
what the nose knows
and baleful eyes hope

at the outdoor pool
seagulls vie for table scraps.
one's feathers ruffle
into a punk Mohawk do.
he's got a punk swagger too.

bottom of the fifth,
coffee tepid now —
still, robin's on deck,
scratching at the mound
of the new flower bed

too small and mealy
to warrant picking for pie,
for cider or wine,
but the waxwings and finches
lift hearts from heavy branches

stems still attached,
these little green apples
litter the lawn:
the fuse-that-through-the-flower
gone þffft in the wind

Chainlink Tanka
for the Jerk Next Door

Our neighbour hates cats,
wants ours off his property
or else he'll bait traps —
as if cats understand yards,
the terrible leash of words.

    *

I tell him if he
so much as touches our cats,
I'll beat him senseless,
and we bark at each other
over the back fence.

    *

The guy's an asshole
surrounded by cat lovers,
thinks ours are the ones
responsible for the shit
he finds in his flower beds.

    *

Maybe I should coil
a mainspring on his front lawn,
gather our dog's shit,
fling it on his roof one night,
tell him it's airplane flushings.

    *

We're responsible:
the cats are both neutered, nice.
they don't caterwaul,
get into battle royals
the way the two of us do.

*

Carotids bulging,
we strain at our own leashes,
want nothing so much
as the opportunity
to rip each other's throats out.

bergamot's bolted —
blossoms at their nadir now;
still, the last bees
are busy as candy stripers
among the pink petals

Canada Day —
in the sky above the lake
chrysanthemum blooms
and umbrella tracer plumes;
old guy rhymes with July

megaphone blooms
of the day lilies blare
while a butterfly flutters —
white-gloved hands
above a cocktail glass

little windfall apples —
green cherry bombs,
each with unlit fuse,
litter the lawn between us,
and here come the ants

(for Rob and Gloria)

among windfall wasps
one stalwart butterfly
spreads its wings:
even the sodden lawn chair
offers expirant heat

at the farthest reach
of my watering
hose stream
a cabbage white
flutters a while

at Chapters —
a friend's survival memoir
greets me from the shelves.
a small copper butterfly
hovers over a blossom

Leddy Headbutter —
named after his feline
way with the blues:
I've done carousing. Wake up.
You can pet me, feed me now.

Serious Moonlight

on the lush green strip
under serious moonlight
the thin white duke
of the weeping birch shimmies,
croons into a street lamp

*

the dog, all this time
on a serious snout cruise,
looks up, sees a thin
white wafer in the branches,
waits for the hand that feeds it

twilight ...
and still the ants scurry.
emergency crew
rushing across the tarmac
just after the plane crashes

four pontoon legs splayed
and two oar-like legs to row:
no wasted effort,
water striders merely twitch
to get to where they want to go

(for Karen Hofmann)

waiting for hired help —
these new fence posts
like legionnaires
back in their foxholes
lean into each others' lies

water pressure down,
whirling dervish sprinkler
suddenly a shaman
shaking shakere water
drops on the earth

no carp in the pond?
the pretty tour guide explains
gulls eat all the fish
then poop all over the rocks.
ah! the old turtle smiles too

"As is" ginkgo —
meaning if it dies, oh well,
Canadian Tire
is not responsible
for the eons it's survived

bilobal leaves —
God's catcher's mitt
for the sun's high fly,
or a green butterfly ruse?
ginkgo's leaves circle the trunk

distant raucous jay,
what more can you add
to dachshund's grudging woof?
he can't see you, poor thing;
nor, he knows, can I

dachshund watches wasp
fly a horizontal course
past his pointed snout.
he hesitates to give chase
though his haunches quiver so

dog run path's deep ruts —
retriever and dachshund stop
every few feet
to read The Piss and Scat
Leader Post

with my glasses off
the lamplight is a glowing
dandelion clock!
twenty-three years together,
we step gently off the curb

park bench —
broken pill bottles, butts,
beer can ring;
bench donated by
the Kiwanis Club

"God is Love,"
the cliff paint says —
no petroglyphs,
only the rock shapes
of falling buffalo

(Lundbreck Falls, Alberta)

geraniums blaze
against the dying light
while cosmos sputter,
drop a petal, waiting for
the last butterfly to land

inside, wanting out,
a ladybug putts about
the double-glazed glass,
crosses whole skeins
of thinning cirrus cloud

lamplight dimmer now,
heat waves more visible
than the twin mantles' glow,
but my front yard lamp still burns
this cool, blustery morning

taking off my clothes,
washing up, doing my teeth
by bedside lamplight,
I see the younger woman
you once were smile in her sleep

from Coltrane Pops

Tyner comps under
the silver splash of cymbals,
Coltrane's alley sax
searching paper bags and cans
out in these mean bass streets

 *

Tyner's finch fingers
titter in the cymbal splash
of falling waters
while 'Trane's tenor weeps
of home from a farther shore

 *

rim shot! cymbal splash!
cat's ears pivot toward
the sun-splashed shores.
who's rowing this awful boat
toward the Godhead now?

    *

rim shot! splash!
Trane takes the tiller on tenor,
stars' canopy
acceding passage
to the band's green boat

    *

look out, Jericho!
got an ax that'll blow
leaves off the trees;
gotta blow torch
and acetylene will!

tourists themselves,
mother mallards glide over
the well-trimmed hedge,
motor across the surface
of the meditation pond

a raucous squabble —
cacophony of crow caws
and magpie squawks —
still the flicker's shrill retort
holds the upper branch and scale

a flickering blue light —
distant campfire beckoning?
no, big screen TV
across the street, up the hill,
screened by a curtain of firs

slack tide —
the choice of walking the strand
or doubling back:
a very old, up-turned,
very barnacled boat

(Saanich Inlet, Victoria)

last to leaf out,
the green ash's new growth green
a lime popsicle
to the mind's eye,
whatever notes flicker floats

chrysanthemum moon —
the poet's bald head shines
above his poems.
my reflection wavers
in the leisurely current.

(for Blaine Greenwood)

so many weeds!
I don't wonder that any
half holy man could
walk across these still waters
in a pair of rubber thongs.

so still
even the grass
allows easy passage
of the ant
one blade to another

Mt. Prevost:
A Tanka Suite

(for Pete & Kayla)

no fire warnings —
mushroomy humus
of the forest floor
in my nostrils
brings me home

*

top of the trail
rock and asphalt?
remnants of a wartime
lookout installation
now a hang glider's leap

*

kinnikinnick —
or some relative of
the stately arbutus?
branches highest at
the edge of the cliff

*

Mt. Prevost —
small print of
the hang-gliding rules
at the edge of the cliff
still hard to read

(Mt. Prevost, near Duncan, BC)

crawling into cracks
of the old garden timbers,
bees carry rolled leaves.
blueprints for a nest
or apian wallpaper?

one cirrus smudge
against cornflower blue sky —
only the marshmallow
forms the snow takes
soften the shadows

"Save our elms"—
standard tape around the trunk,
but on the suckers
someone's left a rosary.
to ward off what, I wonder

haikoodling
my wife calls the process —
such a simple term
for such slow slogging
in the word trenches

so hard to tell
whether bird or last leaf
on top the bare elm.
ah, but I prefer bird,
resist binocular proof

long shadows —
sky cornflower blue
just the same.
every snow-capped house
a cupcake today

so cold —
even the frosting
on the fence
remains undisturbed
by paw prints

sick in bed —
from the dresser mirror
staves of the power lines
wait for the grace notes
of the birds' silhouettes

broken branches
bridge between trembling aspen —
plaques and tangles
in winter's own
frozen mind

pine martin tracks —
patterns as distinct
as our snowshoe shuffle:
no hesitation though,
only frozen holes

serious cirrus —
irrigation pivot
one long dinosaur
skeleton splayed
along the horizon

watching mosquitoes
probe fat veins in his arm,
he clenches his fist,
watches their abdomens burst.
more fun than swatting them dead

crawfish claws —
all that's left after gulls
drop them on the walk
and feast on the soft
underbellies and feet

can't decide
whether the plants
in the waiting room
are real or not,
whether it matters

driving my blind
mother-in-law
to the airport —
all the trees in leaf save one
ganglion elm on the plain

so many RVs
up on blocks, for sale;
gas prices so high —
I half expect the tortoise
to divest himself of his shell

old Hammond B —
same price I paid for her
in the sixties:
that, and all the other notes
suddenly so sweet

(for Quenton Wagstaff)

twenty-six years
since Nigeria was home —
my sand-cast statue
Fulani Venus mama
holds court in the flower bed

a sudden zephyr —
the Moorish turban turbine —
the neighbour's roof vent —
spins silver rays' raiment,
draws in Aladdin air

Weedwhacker and Finch —
could be a legal firm,
but, no, it's my
retired barbarian
neighbour making grass meek

chainsaw caterwaul —
no match for robin's
burbling rejoinder.
if this were a cutting contest,
the bird would win wings down!

after the storm
twigs litter the lawn,
magpies come
to size up the lumber
for their nest

hazardous structure
the spillway sign warns;
osprey crying —
to express displeasure
at our human presence

on the windfall gash
a butterfly spreads its wings.
more wine than nectar
still, it siphons what it can
amid the red cheeks and rot

sister too nervous
to drive the freeway
proposes her friend's
uninsured limo service —
its shadow longer than the car

(Sauble Beach, ON)

Riding the Dragon

(for Diane & Gepke)

first annual Dragon Boat Race Festival,
Lethbridge, AB, 2002

dragon boat races —
breast cancer survivors toss
petals on the lake,
pray for their fallen sisters
while witnesses hold their boats

*

"feathering" it's called —
cocking the oar ever so
slightly left or right
to keep the boat straight, on course.
Oh, that treatment were that sure!

*

a rose is a rose —
the team named Chemo Savvy
know it in their bones;
still, their muscles must ache less
when they cross the finish line

    *

stand on the gunwales
the coach advises steersmen —
get part of the blade
out of the water and you
will see better, cut your drag

    *

we're all paddlers here —
those in the dragon boats who
row furiously
against fear's metastases,
those on the sidelines who yell

    *

Dig! Dig! One! Two! Three!
the drummer yells to my mates.
power ten on three…!
I draw a bead from ball cap
to lamp standard peak and hold

        *

Six/sixteen! she yells —
six deep strong strokes followed by
sixteen quicker ones.
engine room, power house lift
us up until we glide free!

NOTES ON "RIDING THE DRAGON"

Most of the poem sequence will be clear from context, but so that the reader can see the literal images more clearly — and their metaphoric and symbolic import — it might be useful to gloss a few terms used.

"*Hold the boat!*" is a command given to paddlers to bury their oars in unison to stop the forward movement of the boat on a dime; in a sense, we're all inspired to do that by the bravery of breast cancer survivors who choose to buck conventional wisdom and challenge themselves physically after rounds of chemo and invasive surgery.

Feathering is a way of maintaining a steady straight course with minimal movement on the part of the steersman. S/he rotates the paddle a few degrees left or right without reefing on the oar and that compensates for any unevenness in the paddlers' strokes.

Engine room and power house are the literal terms — obviously metaphoric — for the different sections of paddlers responsible for the steady steam and extra power the rowers provide.

The dragon boat is a long, narrow canoe-like boat that carries 18 or 20 paddlers in nine or ten rows of two rowers each. The drummer calls the rhythm and sits facing the paddlers from the stern, seated behind the dragon's head. The steersman stands — I call him the "vulgar boatman" — in back before the tail with a single long steering oar. The first three rows set the rhythm and the drummer takes her cue from them, calling the moves and hitting the drum accordingly. The next three or four rows are the engine room — bigger, stronger oarsman in wider seats. The last group are the terminators (my power house), and they are the first gear, so to speak: slowly paddling the boats into the starting gate, and performing functions as called upon by the drummer or steersman, as required in docking and setting a course.

About the Author

Richard Stevenson is the author of 23 full-length books and 7 chapbooks, including, most recently, *Bye Bye Blackbird*, *The Emerald Hour*, *Tidings of Magpies*, and *Wiser Pills*. He holds degrees in English and Creative Writing from the University of Victoria and University of British Columbia, and teaches at Lethbridge College in southern Alberta.